Whispers from Her Deathbed

Whispers from Her Deathbed

A Posthumous Poetry Collection

by Janavi Held

Edited by Catherine L. Schweig

2022

GOLDEN DRAGONFLY PRESS

AMHERST, MASSACHUSETTS

FIRST PRINT EDITION, June 2022
FIRST EBOOK EDITION, July 2022

Cover art by © Landis Blair
Layout by Alice Maldonado
Set in Brioso Pro and Garamond Pro

"After" originally appeared in *Eternal: Award Winning Poetry* anthology
edited by Ted Stanley and published by Hammond House.

ISBN: 978-1-7370545-2-8

Library of Congress Control Number: 2022939231

Printed on acid-free paper supplied by a Forest Stewardship Council-certified
provider. First published in the United States of America by Golden Dragonfly
Press, 2022.

www.janaviheld.com

www.goldendragonflypress.com

"Time I am,
the great destroyer of the worlds,
and I have come here to destroy all people."

BHAGAVAD GITA

"Love existed before heaven or earth,
Love's presence is not from our time."

HAFIZ

Contents

I

II

III

"A woman in harmony with her spirit is like a river flowing. She goes where she will without pretense and arrives at her destination prepared to be herself, and only herself."

MAYA ANGELOU

Foreword

Janavi was named after a river. "My namesake flows through a land I have never seen, but which feels like home to me…" Here, Janavi speaks of a tributary of the world's largest and most fertile river delta: the Ganges Delta—originating in the snowy mountain tops of Tibet and Nepal, flowing down through Bangladesh and India, and finally, emptying out into the Bay of Bengal. Janavi continues: "…She cannot be contained by dams. In her, sacred dancing myth and true stories collide."

On the shores of "myth and true stories," Janavi's artistic spirit flowed forth from her heart, most uninhibitedly, as a mighty river of poetry. In the last fifteen years of Janavi's life, literally hundreds and hundreds of poems broke her dam. One of the main catalysts for this roaring outpour was, as she put it: "Having an illness that brought me close to death…"

The ancient and exotic story surrounding Janavi's namesake tells of a wildly flowing, celestial river that was temporarily detained in the cosmos. When the river finally splashed down to Earth, she did so with such exuberance that her waters inundated the sacrificial grounds of a great sage, or rishi, known as Janu. Unsettled by this, Janu—of mystical might—swallowed the whole river in one sip, trapping her once again in his Himalayan cave.

But the river—then known as the Ganges—wasn't meant to spend the rest of her life swirling inside Janu's cavernous body. So, she escaped through the sage's ear, rushing down the mountain in several streams, so no one could ever again stop her flow. That day, the Himalayas appeared to grow long white locks of hair, as the river's whitewater rapids trickled down the mountain's sides, sustaining all who drank from it. Henceforth, the mighty river was also known as 'Jhanavi.'

In the spring of 2004, as Janavi completed her thirty-ninth year, her health dwindled to the point that she had to lay to rest her dream of pursuing a career in dance. In digging a grave for her budding dance career, Janavi experienced a dramatic existential shift within herself, which she describes as such: "…my perspective on life had been profoundly altered, and I was becoming aware that no matter how safe staying-put may seem, I would not be able to continue. I felt something pushing from the inside—a voice so certain that I had no choice but to follow along." That inner catalyst moved Janavi to sell her studio, give away most of her belongings, and lend herself entirely to healing, to communing with Nature—which she related to as "the highest expression of The Divine here on Earth," and to following her creative impulses, which emerged, primarily, as poetry: her life's breath.

Janavi's poetry wasn't only the breath that sustained her in her final years, but, ironically so, also a beautiful and brave death narrative, through which she learned to embrace dying, as a natural and integral part of life. For most of us, the exact time of our death remains a mystery. For others—especially those with chronic, potentially terminal illnesses, like Janavi—death's shadow often becomes a companion, a reminder that our existence here is fragile and fleeting.

The fragility of Janavi's health condition, and how she coped with it, gracefully spilled into her poems as we hear her praying "for sleep on endless nights", feeling alone, "longing to be reassembled," and calling out to a divine surgeon from her sickbed: "You are my surgeon, for I am ill—sick with the disease of eons… I hear Your surgeon's tools rattling in the dawn shadows."

The "disease of eons," as per the Vedic texts Janavi treasured, was the illusion that though we see everyone around us dying, we resist pondering our own inevitable death. To ancient indigenous cultures around the world—like the ones sustained by the River Jahnavi in India—denial of death, or fear of it, was regarded as a highly undesirable state of being, frequently described as a tight flower bud refusing to blossom, or stagnant water unable to flow. Janavi's mighty river of creativity was anything but that! And the plethora of poems she left behind is an inspiring testament to that.

While putting together Janavi's posthumous poetry collection, I drew primarily from poetry Janavi composed over the last fourteen years of her life, as she struggled with the insidious illness that plagued her. With guidance from Janavi's own poetry files—and the meticulous manner in which she had organized them—I dove into the oceanic body of work she left behind, (including four completed chapbooks) and surfaced with 65 carefully selected treasures, in a nod to her birth year: 1965.

The book's title, *Whispers from Her Deathbed*, was borrowed, in part, from the title of one of Janavi's unfinished poetry manuscripts. The collection is divided into three sections, which, Janavi described as such: "Time and how it relates to nature, how time influences our bodies and our social circumstances, and the perception of time and how it influences our spiritual evolution." Janavi drew the theme—on time and the subjectivity of time—from a verse in the *Bhagavad Gita*, where exploring time, paradoxically, illuminates what it's like to exist *outside* of time. A journey which ultimately carried her beyond "landscapes of flesh and steel," toward how to understand "the original stuff we are made of."

Lost in time, in the changing sky outside her bedside window in Colorado, Janavi exclaims in one of her poems, as she dictates into her laptop: "I didn't know that time could drag on like this, through pain." When the passing of time becomes synonymous with pain, the two merge into one very powerful teacher, with whom Janavi became very close. Shaped, as such, by her never-ending experience of pain, Janavi's poems spontaneously became a dialogue with pain, and time, and, also, with death—as the point in time when her intense physical pain would end.

In the last poems Janavi wrote, she expresses having been "chased by pain" for years, and in "Pain's Purpose" reveals a longing for what she calls "the restless sweetness at the end of time." In her final poetic offerings, Janavi speaks of wishing for wings, soaring through "mists of bright clouds," bathing in moonlight, drinking in the dust of stars. She pictures her heart filling with "ancient light" as she looks… "down at the swarming earth, but never…back." Then, in the poem Janavi titled "After"— which was shortlisted for the prestigious Hamilton House International Poetry Prize, and appeared in their anthology titled 'Eternal'— Janavi simply asks: "After death, *what*?."

I know a fresh tomb awaits me
among a host of tangled vegetation.
I know that my superstitious heart
lives among trees and fading flowers.

In the last four months of her life, Janavi reached out to both friends and family, and at other times appeared to push them away, as she withdrew into the ancient Sanskrit texts containing the story of her namesake. There, she resonated with the words of Queen Kunti, known for enduring indescribable pain. In the end, it was this pain that moved the queen to compose 26 poetic verses in which she wishes for her focus to shift from her own inescapable painful circumstances to the Divine. Janavi's favorite was: "O Lord of Madhu, as the Ganges forever flows to the sea without hindrance, let my attraction be constantly drawn unto You, without being diverted to anyone else" (*Bhagavat Purana* 1.8.42).

As Janavi understood it, this mysterious sea that unfolds entirely beyond time's perimeters is eternal space, "where all speech is song, and all walking, dance" (*Sri Brahma Samhita*, 5.56). And a place she inevitably begins nearing, in her poetic, ontological stroll past the dualities of living and dying. In the pages that follow, you'll encounter the musings of Janavi's very youthful and exuberant spirit: naturally longing to dance, yet confined within a painful body that inhibited dancing. This juxtaposition between forces of restraint vs. urges to release, is a theme woven throughout Janavi's poetry, as it was in the genesis story of the River Jahnavi, who continues giving of her waters, to this day.

In her own story, Janavi lovingly imbibes her namesake, leaving us—and future generations—to quench our thirst at her river of poems, expressing: "...I realize that the best kind of dying is that dying which gives new life to others." In writing unapologetically about her imminent demise, unwilling to compromise the course of the creative rivers that rushed from her heart, Janavi also gifts us an opportunity to let our own tight buds blossom, our stagnant waters flow.

Today, as you drink from her river of poems, you may discover that Janavi's honest poetry doesn't try to be pretty, and yet, it is, in its straightforwardness, especially, as we hear her whisper a final wish to us from her deathbed: "I want the cool embrace of sacred rivers flowing on my skin, the dancing of peacocks... true friends chanting of eternity next to my ears." And, perhaps, if we listen carefully enough, we may also hear her finally flowing into the tranquil sea.

Catherine L. Schweig
Newport News, Virginia

*"While I thought that I was learning how to live,
I was learning how to die."*

LEONARDO DA VINCI

Introduction
by Janavi Held

I asked myself, how do I begin? How do I find a voice so long discarded—covered by the doubt that this act of creation may have no value—when survival is pressing down on me like an impending winter storm? How do I begin the act of discovering what my authentic dharma is—my purpose in life—when I have been taught not to trust my own instincts?

By putting pen to paper, that's how. Without intention, but only propelled by a growing need for imagination; this is where I began to muster the courage to discard a life, so long in tatters, for the flickering sensation that there is something else I can do.

My mother once told me, "If you want to write well, write what you know." This is what I know: People want to be happy. They want to live satisfying and fulfilling lives. They want to be valued and loved. But the nature of modern life can distort these natural tendencies and, as we pursue an artificial pace of life, we pursue desires that may not be our truest desires or in our best interest, and we fall deeper and deeper into the trap of modern soullessness, as our soul's voice gets buried.

The most extraordinary irony is that it takes time and contemplation, long walks and soulful conversations with friends to excavate that voice, to hear its particular needs underneath the cacophony of modern life. Are we moving at too fast a pace to think deeply about the true condition of our existence? Deep thought takes time. There are things that take time to understand. Perhaps it is within the deep stillness—beneath the surface of life—that the soulful voice can be found, which can then lead us to a more soulful and honest manner of living.

As a child, I lived with a deep curiosity, a profound love of the natural world. I was restless, enthusiastic, and determined, which made me throw myself, heart and soul, into whatever intrigued me at the moment. I loved to create and had a natural talent for organizing the elements, components, or tools of creativity, whatever they were at the moment.

But also, when I was very young, I had a severe case of dyslexia. My world did not co-operate in the way that it did for other children. As I began to learn that my perceptions of things in my environment were not "accurate" perceptions, I began to build my castles in the air—my creations in imaginative flight—because this was the only environment I was comfortable in. It was the only environment where nobody could tell me that I had done something wrong.

I've never been able to describe what those early years were like, but some time ago I came across a book called *The Gift of Dyslexia*, which so accurately described the way that I saw and experienced the world as a child that it startled me. In part, because often a dyslexic child is taught that how she imagines her world is inaccurate, and so hearing another person articulate what I was experiencing was refreshing. And I began to think, perhaps it wasn't wrong at all, perhaps it was just *different*.

We are all different from each other in our own unique ways, and we are all, also, the same. I believe that within each of us there is a map to humanity at large. In telling my story I hoped to discover all those elements—internal and external—that led me to reclaiming my creative voice, and thereby, to living a more authentic life. It is living authentically which has, ultimately, brought me to a deeper connection to humanity at large. It is through this inner journey that I have awakened a fresh compassion for my fellow humans—compassion that began with taking a compassionate look at myself.

In early spring of 2004, I crawled into the back of a storage closet in my home in Boulder, Colorado and dragged out a metal trunk that a friend had brought back from India, which had become a place to store all manner of artifacts, including my old writings. That day, I read through a plethora of poems that I wrote in my late teens and flipped through seemingly endless piles of journals. "Where is my pen and paper?" I wondered, as I drifted off to sleep. I then dreamt of walls and doors crumbling—disintegrating by the touch of my hand—and I walked for miles collecting stones, leaves and shells until my pockets were overflowing.

The next morning, I found an aging notebook, blank, yet with tattered pages and an obliging pen. On that memorable day, the atmosphere around me—interpreted through my newly awakened senses—appeared more vivid. The air was pregnant with spring rain, echoing on my roof, waking up the dormant green that hides itself during the winter months. I felt moved to walk into the downpour, to feel the texture of moisture on my skin, to see how the earth breathes, moves, and wakes in the new spring air.

Thoroughly wet, I touched the ground with my feet watching the unfolding sky release fast moving crystals of rain. Intuition awakened within, and my feet knew which direction to tread, which location to seek as my life suddenly opened on that foggy morning.

Returning home, I reached for that tattered notebook and wrote with a new certainty about the unmet longing that had cowered helplessly in my heart during years of unlived potential. My life had shrunk down to a distorted shape, a shape informed by the can-nots and the should-nots of society. It resembled the quiet grave of a two-year-old child I saw once in a decaying graveyard: so much potential unmet, cut short, and there sat the epitaph two hundred years from her death. I wept quietly as I read her short life story wondering how I got so lost.

When did I put down the words that had carried my heart to waking? When did the path away from creativity become appealing to my feet? I think 'survival' was the name of that road, and so my feet are not to blame. Perhaps a temporary journey away from self is part of the path to find that self.

As I sat writing, I thought that this is the best place I can be right now: closest to Divinity, gazing at the divine shapes of my unfolding heart. Letting her speak what is most true and what is—like my soul—ever fresh and as vast as time and space, all pouring out in my poems. I was once told that poetry is "the language of God."

For days and months, I rode the wave of poetry emanating from my heart, blood, and mind, as if a dam had broken. The moments of my life translated into poetry, and the past was there as well as every pain, every joy, every bit of life in her garments of confusion and bitterness. Her enigmatic effigy stood bold on the pages I caressed with my pen.

Each morning as I opened my eyes words poured out like a violent and reckless stream running over her banks. At night, the words sounded like the crashing waves of the Pacific Ocean ripping through my dreams. Some nights the poems would not let me sleep; I sat up late as they dictated their long stories dancing loudly across hundreds of pages of clear, white paper. Endless words rolled and lingered in my mind, dreaming me back to life.

I am amazed by the creative process. During this spontaneous process of creation, I felt that my hardest work was just to let it gestate, let it sit in that quiet formless space in between waking and sleeping, and in between history and future. Sometimes it's bewildering how long a creative project can gestate before it is ready to be born, and then how it suddenly comes pouring out, taking form so confidently. It is hard to imagine that it was once just a thought, just elements, atoms, particles of emotion and imagination born from experience, born from just the simple task of living these days on Earth.

In *The War of Art*, Steven Pressfield argues for the existence of the angelic muse, who resides over pen and paintbrush, over the dancer's body, and the actor's words:

> "....when we sit down day after day and keep grinding, something mysterious starts to happen. A process is set into motion by which, inevitably and infallibly, heaven comes to our aid, unseen forces enlist in our cause; serendipity reinforces our purpose.... The muse takes note of our dedication. She approves. We have earned favor in her sight. When we sit down and work, we become like a magnetized rod that attracts iron filings. Ideas come. Insights accrete."

And so, it is with me. Not only do I feel the force of that angel whispering as I create, I also see her in the images of other photographers, the strokes of a painter's brush, the movements of a dancer's body, the vocabulary of a poet, and in the faces of friends and family. I see her in the stars of the autumn sky, inside the ether, the flowers and grass, in the eyes of animals, and within all the dreams I've ever had. They gather with me as I write these words, collecting themselves silently into inspiration, transforming gradually into the products of creation.

One of my favorite expressions of this sense of collecting inspiration is in a line from a song called *For a Dancer*, by Jackson Browne, "Just do the steps that you've been shown by everyone you've ever known until the dance becomes your very own."

What is my own dance, exactly? Classifying my poetry into a particular genre is a difficult task for me. Yet on deeper reflection, I see that I would be most comfortable putting myself in the same category as writers who see the artistic journey as a means of healing and personal evolution, of living life in a more soulful manner. A shift of one's individual awareness, growth, and personal responsibly is often at the root of communal or global change. In my own life, I can see how a shift in my inner landscape over time has dramatically changed my outer landscape.

As an artist—an individual particularly interested in excavating that authentic voice and living in a harmonious manner with the Earth, and my community, I have, through this creative adventure, endeavored to find my own pace with which to move through my remaining days on Earth: a slower pace. Anything that emerged from this became my offering to the many muses I've had in my life, who taught me simply *to listen* and to have the courage to follow my authentic path, regardless of the fashion of the moment.

I've realized that what led me to this burning desire to give myself to the creative path and live a more authentic life was something much deeper: a renaissance of soul. The experience of doing so has taught me that the greatest remedy for this modern ill of soullessness is not only greater time spent in the natural world, but a recognition that She has much to teach us about ourselves and about how to manage the pace and rhythm of our lives. I believe that Nature is the highest expression of The Divine here on Earth, and my poetry, I think, reflects this.

When I was suddenly struck by a painful illness, I spontaneously sought the earth, flowers, and sun for comfort. I prayed, lying on her warm lap, in Divinity's natural cathedral, gazing at the clear blue sky, the ceiling built by sacred hands, flowers—creepers drying in the December sun, my only companions, pretty pages in the book of my life.

Although I had no idea where I would find myself at the end of my creative journey of authentic, artistic expression, I always knew that, in the end, it would take the form of a book. This is because I have always loved books! Even before I could read.

I feel uncomfortable in a house with no books; a lack of books seems to make the air nervous. As a publisher's daughter, I grew up with books—books in shelves, in boxes in the hall, piled up by the front door, in the basement, delivered by the truckload fresh from the printer. I love the smell of a newly-made book. An old familiar book is comforting, like a pair of broken-in jeans or shoes. New books, whether fact or fiction, hold the promise and thrill of undiscovered territory.

Books are beautiful, even when they're not: color, texture, shape, size, font, paintings, drawings, cover art, content, theme, story, information! A beautiful compact piece of art using a plethora of artistic disciplines. I found that a new book could become a comforting old friend very quickly as I began the intimate act of touching and turning each thin page, as the book gave up its most intimate secrets.

Books are like people to me: so much to learn, discover, and unfold. It takes time to know a book or a person. You must invest effort and possess imagination to enter into a relationship with them—books and people alike! You must accept them as they are, suspend disbelief, and take them at face value, although you may not agree with everything they say.

While bedridden, I experienced a profound sense of feeling separate from everything and everyone. When there is so much pain in the body, and it becomes immobile, it feels akin to being buried alive in a glass tomb. At such times, I'd see the world around me, interact with others, and yet there was always the sting of loneliness. As I lay in bed, I dreamt, at first, of days past, walking in the fresh spring air watching all manner of life bloom after the cold winter had given way. I mused over so many sweet summers, wondering, praying: will I be a part of it all again? Will I ever reenter the dance?

I knew later, much later, that the answer to that question was no, and that I had to find my true self: the one that lives on after the body dies. I knew the time had come to relocate my dreams to my inner landscapes, to instead frolic among the inner flower gardens, search out that place where there is no time. And so, my poems, inevitably, began to explore the concept of time, and exiting time, and doing so at peace.

The Jackson Brown lyrics continue: "No matter how close to yours another's steps have grown, in the end, there is one dance you'll do alone."

✳ ✳ ✳

(The latter Introduction was pieced together by prose Janavi Held composed in the final years of her life, together with excerpts from her 50-page thesis titled "Days on Earth: Creativity and a Journey of Reclamation," submitted in 2009, toward the Bachelor of Arts degree she received from Goddard College.)

I

"To see a world in a Grain of Sand,
And a Heaven in a Wild Flower,
Hold Infinity in the palm of your hand,
And Eternity in an hour."

WILLIAM BLAKE

"I believe that Nature is the highest expression
of The Divine here on Earth,
and my poetry, I think, reflects this."

JANAVI HELD

It's Time

I saw a plum tree dressed in full paisley
blossoms,
and although the wind touched my
cheeks
with cool fingers,
I felt the sun high
overhead,
breaking through the billowing,
unattached air.

It is time to stop peeling open the
various wounds
of long-ago yesterdays:
let that spring-like evolution
bring young skin to cover those
blistering memories,
let a well-earned amnesia transform
dried memories
into food for tomorrow's nutrition.

Perhaps it is time to sleep,
even when old nightmares threaten
the sanctity of rest,
even when I cannot walk forward
properly just yet,
even when the fog of this cold spring
still shrouds the horizon
and makes invisible the painted sky.

Spring

Nameless
My breath mixes with blue
And delirious summer diamonds
Those flowers

The heart of the earth
Bite into sunshine
Like the unfailing sting of rain
Warm color of mountains and wind

Warlike, always new
According to the almanac
Keeping track of ploughed lands
And vines

That keep moving to the sky
Up where pollen flies
And silence is victorious.
Ether, laden with the waves

Of twilight
Garlands the mortal chain
With endless impermanence.
Spring brings hope

Eyes watch
The forgotten dregs of winter
Following death
Where life takes her.

Flaming city of western sunset
Like hubris and tears
Darkens constellations
Of primitive aberrations

Of the exploding sounds
Of unspoken dawns
Growing from the anniversary
Of so many daybreaks

And the flesh of man falls
The ocean awaits his blood
At the edge of civilization
Reciting the testimony of flowers

And farewell cities
Of thwarted legacies.
A tyrant
With mortal eyes

Feasts on the memory of angels
Inheriting their repose.
And after this
Spring returns

Violent as birth
The steel of winter has gone
Warmth is an explosion

The Language of Rain

Rain keeps plunging
in its sun stealing shapes
as grey shadows
take away the depth
of my sky blue.

Foggy messes
blanket me
in moist quiet.

Here,
noise is disguised
by languishing water drops
everything disappearing
into a satin sheet of weather
covering minds in introspection
and at home desires
fall into place.

That air,
heavenly air
carries my desire
to be in it
all the time
no indoor tomb for me.

I wish the rain
to never stop
and perpetually bring
these crazy July winds

always wet
through my ever-open windows.
Thunder comes
on the heels of water
asking me to pay attention
waking me
to outside fragrances
reminding me where I was born.

As a resident of this earth
I know
it is raining for me
because I have been dry
for too long.

Exterminated Rock

Only
the blue
of the sky
is left

to mourn
and remember
departed days
of earth

and salty things.
Her memory
is like volcanic weeping,
idols of milk,

and frost,
and stone
sunken now
in exhausted shadows,

and the menacing metal
of steel
like ice,
like accidental death,

or an absent mother
with cloudy memories.
The shadow
of seasons

caress the solitary shore
as the rise
and fall
of people sink

like a forgotten army
even when the twilight air
is laden with hope,
like the heavy scent

of jasmine flowers;
time
will have her victory.
Even the aviators of night

cannot chain their machines
to immortality;
the mortal coil
consumes nails

that bind flesh
to spirit,
and according to atoms
they are ploughed under,

fertilizing the next
generation
of hands and eyes,
and no one remembers.

Iron Age

I am indifferent to these days
As they pass like iron.
Balconies built with hands of stone
Stumble from their observatory
Resembling the shattered metal of oblivion.
Accumulated phantoms speak
In hushed lamentation
As the violence of newborn life
Breaks the iron thunder of death.

The ancient wisdom of philosophers
Lays like mulch in the suffocated earth
Today those roses rot slowly
Impaled by their own thorns
As the flogged memory of these ancestors
And that philosopher's stone
Like honey, drips,
With a newly developed
Synthetic taste.

The natural wind is confused,
And with shattered lips it arrives in the evening
Covered with the vague belly of death
Overturning all our perfectly polished plastic and steel.
Carbon, now extruded from earth, iron is invisible.
And so, the corpse of the wind overturns
Our mechanized creations
But cannot digest these shattered parachutes
As they drag like violent kisses.

Synthetic structures
Battle the philosopher's stone for blood,
Strictly following the lawlessness
Of submerged factories,
And that ether climbs and climbs,
Searching for that circle of worn away dreams,
Oozing violent strands of air
As the wraith-like philosophers watch
With lightning bolt eyes.

Wardrobe

Clouds throb in the distant waking light
branches tremble
endless harmony with the heavy wind
pale, still light meandering
through this unending bit of cold
gradually does the light arise
not like the stagnant minutes of perception.

In watching I have unearthed time
resurrected the sweetness of the sun
I have been looking at the same thing
for an eternity
have made legends out of flowers
and the soft moving trees.
as the horizon, so out of control
is conceited by its own freedom
this vertiginous stretch
of anonymous land.

I would move in many directions
at once if I could stop feeling like a transparent midnight.
Instead I stand silent in the center of my thoughts
watching the clouds enter and move away
watching bridges built to collapse
watching the words claim space
reflecting on obscenities
like death and illness.

My wardrobe is made from
all these tattered thoughts.
Cast away from the living
I embody what no one
wants to know.

Time Unhinged

Dreamt of exterminated images,
and forgotten doubts,
of unhinged time
with the hollow

of silent bones
thundering
in the wake of restless flowers.
Blinded by

a vigilant morning
I enter the mists of loneliness
seeking laughter and daydreams
(to counter the emptiness)

too long for counting
these days
press down
on my chest,

cementing the architecture
of my sad inheritance.
I establish hope
burying her under

the obliging tree
in my back yard.

All of It

I have a notion
of time before
I was polluted with tears.
A time when my dreams
were stolen by my muse
and sent to ripen in The Painted Sky.
And today I have no other lover.

I don't remember
if all lost yesterdays were better,
but I love the green of growing things all the more:

the trembling roots of it all
showing their daggers and the thorns of it all
and bark stripped like bleeding skin
and the sadness of it all
and the sap like blood trickling from endless wounds
and the knives, that sharpen in the stomach of the mountains
and the endlessness of it all
like winter wind
and cold with no compassion
and the anger of it all
and the tears of it all
and the endless birth and death of it all
with no remorse
and the sleep of it all
and the illness of it all.

Roots

Discarded longings
penetrate the silence
like lightning
reminding me of
yesterday's earthquakes
and unwanted passions
which tear the roots
out of my silence
the dregs of dismantled
intentions beg for time
and I am here
just here thickening
in the shadow
of yesterday's dreams.

Going Home

Oh, wind you cannot comfort me!
For I have listened to your voice alone for too long now
and pools of abstract tears have fallen in piles around my drowning feet.

I can't comfort you as you stray from tree to tree,
can't call your violent names when the darkness of the night
covers even the fullest moon;
she is like me pulling on the tides—undecided.

I can't speak to you anymore
because literal thoughts have eaten the tongue out of my mouth;
as handfuls of pebbles—soft river stones—clatter to the ground
after years of being collected with my hands,
they drop randomly now,
going home.

Sunset Walking

Exposed bones of trees
nestle into dirt

soaking in pink rays
of a restless evening

veins of leaves cling
to frozen branches

resting under the silence of snow
wandering

my eyes
have been entrusted

with all this glamour
my vision cares for it

as best it can
consuming only

what's necessary
for survival.

Sweet

Sweet, the air.
I, in repose
drink this breath.
There is still life
drifting into my window.

The Prince of Clocks

Here
sensations are much closer
to soul-like places
than days with hours
and clocks
against God's will.

A poet
cannot get stuck
languishing
in her box
of clocks
and watches
and appointments.

If I could have my way
clocks would depart
to dreams
and calendars
would empty
their numbers
into the weather systems
of each month
and I would truly discover
what time is
defined broadly
in soul terms.

And so
the prince of clocks
surrenders his arms
to my hands

and gives up
all other seeing.

Reckless thoughts
abandon routines
finding that missing data
which draws bodies
to their treasure of eternity:
timeless schedules.

Somewhere in Time

One cannot estimate greatness
by mundane calculations
like the moon
and her tides
moving sand from here to there
(like me)
making shapes on the shore
indentations
that wash away
at any moment.

Somewhere in time
the ironic sound of analogue static
took the place of the sea's wild noise
which used to keep her company
during dreams of growing up,
growing old,
growing away.

Ignoring the Passage of Days

The birds don't know
that today is a holiday
they still flutter about
searching the December snow
for bits and pieces
of seeds and old fruits and twigs
diligently they work
ignoring the passage of days
and all the meaning we subscribe to them
all the entrances and exits
do not exist in their world
we here, incubate our sorrow
with thoughts and the articles of others
their speech and the impossible echo
resounding in the history
of everything
that once was sentient.

When

Whenever the future finds me
when memory is gone
when longing no longer reminds me
that remaining here is wrong.

When the night tells me
that all this romance is done
when all along I've known You
and memory is long.

When air castles lose their altitude
when roaming the moors of time
when I am lost in attitude
thinking everything is mine.

When You and I can talk again
face to face, as in the lasting land
when You and I take time again
to remind me who I am.

When memory goes out walking
out in the fields of time
when I make my life for Your liking
and can't remember what is mine.

When oceans lose their salt
and I am swimming deep
in the autumn twilight, staying
where I can no longer sleep.

When all the world around me
does not resemble time
when souls animate the foundry
of this everlasting ride.

II

"Time is but the stream I go a-fishing in.
I drink at it; but while I drink I see the sandy bottom
and detect how shallow it is. Its thin current
slides away, but eternity remains."

HENRY DAVID THOREAU

"This part of myself was not a gentle breeze,
but more like a hurricane that would have its way,
regardless. I would have to follow wherever it led me."

JANAVI HELD

Rented Body

I live uneasily
in my rented body
wondering when
the surrogate season
of shadows will pass.
Perishable memories
I have clutched
within this rented vessel;
so many forsaken treasures
slip like blinded angels
through the atoms
of my rented jail.
They do not land on rock;
they come from my bones
like a hurricane,
as my rented flesh is uplifted
by hunger and money
as the two parts
of my soul search for eyes,
for the waterfall,
for the forget-me-nots
to thaw the frozen atmosphere of tears,
for the pale cathedral of doubt
to replace its dead shadow
with a constant heart.
In my rented body
I climb titanic,
twisting stairs,
casting my own shadow
on the torn remnants
of these days,
and mortal fibers,

I've torn them
from my rented heart,
those gentle atoms
living as the symbol
of silence,
of forever,
of the Master
of all destroyed things.

Oxygen

Absentmindedly
my lungs take in oxygen,
and my fingernails grow,
and my heart circulates life
through my careless limbs.
I am entangled in a computer of flesh,
like flowers growing
or vines finding obliging trees
to hug and cling to.
Bits of flesh are adulterous,
eaten by earthly time
as eternity looms longingly,
waiting for me to become a bride,
to pry myself from this blanket of forgetfulness,
this perpetual winter of exasperated cold.
But today, I am still a damp leaf
needing to be sun dried,
still a yellow poppy
or a purple iris needing earth,
and my absentminded lungs remain
silently chewing on God's oxygen.

Bodies of Time

In so many years
have I become nothing

but a curator of time
and circumstance?

Stacking spent minutes in storage
for use in another place.

If I remain a victim
of clocks and watches

how will eternal time
ever get through?

My hands are not strong enough
to pull back the layers

of these fused atoms
or to keep the clock from

defining my personality.
It watches how my body moves,

and thinks, and talks.
That clock takes notes,

building a fabricated version
of my personality.

The eyes of strangers
also engage in this blindness

building notions of my character
with stories from another life.

These clocks and people
see only my fugitive skin.

I am not skin.
I try to live in the small spaces

in between people's eyes,
and the hands of the clock,

and the calculation of eons,
outside of that momentary place

where corporeal eyes clutter my consciousness
with misguided forms of knowing.

Purpose

I do not wish to sit
any longer
behind
shuttered windows
obscuring my view.
Outside,
wind will wash against
my skin
brushing away regret.
Time passed,
choking purpose,
returning passion is
beyond containment:
spilling out
of control.
Time and reason—
self-built dams
shatter.
In healing waters
a dismantled life
seeks a vessel.

Traffic

On quiet days
I live inside
Forsaking the traffic
That lives
Everywhere else.
The voice of ancient scriptures
Interpreted through time
And other languages
Keeps company with my thoughts.
We sing together
Worshipping intuition
And the relevance
Of timely renunciation.
Shadows retreat
Filling silent corners
With occupational whispers.
My heart requests
Not to be called back
To the thick world
Of traffic.

Suburban America

At the edge of an American life
I walk the suburbs,
I eat leftover efforts,
and surf the digital columns of time.

I am recklessly lost in history
planning to escape there
when the wheels stop turning forward
and the traffic is silent.

I walk the suburbs
standing still at times
looking for archeological remnants
of a neglected past.

I am walking the trails of suburban America
and I can't grow the old ways
this is my inheritance.
I have arrived here

by way of a forgotten past,
journeyed on the back
of noisy history,
in the presence of the absent ones

who likely drowned
in the suburbs as well.

Yesterday

Time melts,
thoughts stick,
energy steps
slowly.
Wounds melt,
knowing.
Answers blend,
fog questions
time's relevance.
An old delight
remembers time
living deep in bones.
Yesterday speaks
louder still
and brain waves deliver
restless names
into the cleaver embrace
of today's dignity.
Endless todays, endless todays.

To Love in Time

To love in time
I would have to forget:
that everything turns to mud
even the blood

that flushes your cheeks
and the features and curves
of your skin.
What is left to love

is a facsimile of
a well-worn hero
with broad shoulders
and dashing eyes

moving in and
out of favor
with the hands of time
in and out

of my favor
as I
move on
to prettier flavors

because
even the roundness
and dark of your eyes
has no unlimited home

no everlasting ride.
I tire of you
as passion turns
to the existential tide.

Not even the turn of your cheek
not even the way you move
in the afternoon light
is here forever. Right?

If I get lost
in the momentary thought
that I could be
a pretty wife

my skin reminds me
of the turning stars
they last so much longer
than this momentary life.

Tele-vision

I don't want to remember
  static images crackling with robust electric combustion;
    nor do I wish to see smooth, inhuman, digital TV faces
      speaking of war, and watching bombs explode
        over Baghdad and Afghanistan, a hotel burning in Mumbai,
          a child with shining black skin, bones for limbs and flies for eyes.

I don't want to dream anymore
of riots and dictators, and impersonal imperialism
like the United States of longing and England,
and other places crowned by entitlement.

    I don't want Hollywood stories to cloud my mind's eye
        those regurgitated mythologies and paradox fantasies
    like Cinderella and the boy who was angry and fought for healing.

I want to forget the wholesale humiliation of the common,
the crowning of self-elected kings,
and the eternal nature of genocide and war.

I don't want to be guided by backward intellectualism
  that says stupid is cool
    be misinformed and smoke Kool cigarettes
      and forget what the hippies and beat poets were really saying,
        as they walked away from gold-lined streets,
          and cars, and the slaughter of education,
            and shaken upper-middle class parents
              searching for gurus and timeless time.

I don't want to feed the corporate machine of slavery
consuming inch by inch the planet earth
selling her to the highest bidder

for the latest contraption
that you must have, must have   to be   to be   someone......

        I want the cool embrace of sacred rivers flowing on my skin,
        the dancing of peacocks,
        and true friends chanting of eternity next to my ears.

        I want to remember the green veins of leaves,
        walking in sacred dust
        and eating something that must taste like God.

        I hope for an avalanche of memories of winter storms
        and summer lightning
        like the monsoon blue of sky,
        like God's skin.

        I want to remember the geometry of flowers
        and the creativity of earth's design,
the personalism of trees, and the humility of grass   growing like freedom.

And at last   I want to remember   that   I   am,   that I am
        someone......

Someone

I sit alone on my couch
writing
Someone is dying, being born, crying, laughing, wandering or wondering

I sit alone on my couch
no forward motion
no breathless conversation

I write
sitting alone on my couch

I am languid
I have food in my refrigerator

Someone is scared
Someone has no food to eat

I am happy just watching
the trees outside my window

Someone is climbing
a ladder to success

Someone is dying
unloved in the street
and I am sitting, writing, on my couch

I have floods of memories
as I watch the curtains move with a breeze

Someone has lost track of everything
Someone has no windows

and no time left to breathe.

Self-Indulgence

I die in mirrors.

I eat illusion.

I reflect the sorrow
of arrogance

and feast
on the extremity of fear.

I am fond
of my biography

and the indefinite origins
of disrespect.

Eagerly I ravage
the nutrition

of my heart
and indulge

in digital dreams.

I've broken the heart
of all those who come

to love me.

In this I am persistent.

Dysfunctional

Nocturnal thoughts come like a torrent
a fictitious survivor yellowed by a pilgrimage
to the known world.

Watching the source
a conspiracy is resurrected;
the drought reaches an abrupt end.

Looking at the universe
it is impossible
to know where I am.
I can't see minute things
like organizing my day
around little tasks,
around eating,
making a cup of tea,
going to sleep,
and waking.

And without the minute
I am totally disorientated,
trying to balance my passions
for freedom and organization.

I wait for current minutes to pass—
which contain neither—
because I am looking too closely,
am surrounded by the vastness of the
universe.
It functions…
as I remain dysfunctional.

Chronic Condition Life

Chronic condition life
meandering stark sky
grasping at threads of wisdom

meticulous karma
shapes and shapes
circles and circles

takes away gives
momentarily suffocating
tomorrow's vision

lost in reconciliation
to whatever actions
grow in time

I would forfeit
the chronic condition
for a million nows

not mistaking
the lessons
of history for

anything romantic
for they are nothing
but an effigy of

vice shuddering
in the margin
of assassinated time

that reflection
that carves bracelets
ringing on her wrist

that flesh
that solemn
sacrament squeezes

through an astonished
labyrinth spellbound
worshiping motionless

tragedy pulling
threads through
bloated aspirations

punctuated
in their own
reflection of sobs.

Prideful

Of water and pride,
of descending starlight
and the debilitation of the dawn,
of what consequence are these
when all have endured
the ashen waves of impermanence?

What is the sun to death?
Or the highest peak
of the earth's reach
to the ceaseless bite
of the corruptible serpent?

Stranded on the dying shore,
driven by perpetual secrets
we emerge,
crawling to the endless waves
to look into the abyss,
to open our mouths.

Our secrets appear
and we can't discharge
this corrupt luggage,
it drags eternity down,
dripping through our fingers like wind.

Nothing can grow
in these infertile waves
tarnished with dereliction from duty
and enemies of sense;
it is a frightened paradox,
a rigid spine,

inherited slavery,
a murderer deeply wounded,
frozen rivers,
or falling blood,
burning like oil.

The aristocracy of pride
speaks disdainfully
to the broken siren
of the ecclesiastic night
as heretical syllables sigh
and moan like a restless wraith.

It is faithless
true only to its
promethean masters.
This corrupted angel
inherited by a tangled web of eons

is unmoved
by the blood
flowing
from its own
impartial
pride.

Luxuries

I am not speaking
of disposable income
nor of gold shaped luxuries
nor the inheritance of idle time.

I speak of need.
Of being lost in the desert
one moment from death
and suddenly there is water.

I speak of a child on city streets
whose lonely bones protrude
through sagging skin.
I speak of feeding her.

Because I am
that animal
desert-lost
and that girl-child

with street slackened skin
and longing bones
I can no longer conceal
by day or night.

The luxury of love
cannot be measured
by the libertine
nor by the stopgap

remedies of this
incarceration.
Time measures our activities
and this death-like time

does not concern himself
with our disposable income
nor with our gold shaped
luxuries, and idle time.

The luxury of love
owns eternity
and
nothing more.

Walk

I am alone now
Listening to answers
To the questions
I've posed
To my intuition, my very own
Miniature version of God

I don't always want
To do what I'm told
But the sun keeps
Drawing up over
The eastern horizon
And I keep breathing,

So, faith still settles
Into my renegade bones.
Even though I want to run
You say,
"Running is for later
when you've learned how to walk."

Separate

I am
separate
from
those trees
and
the blue
of sky
longing
I
wait
inside
the blistering
heat
of dawn

Now Gone

the now silent
the now dead

weight of turret and beam
reflects footsteps

now gone
chasms

the impossible
echo

now
gone

shifting memory
like wind

now gone
the possible

the impossible
castle

roads of roses
planted stand
now gone
dignified sun

attic dust
small feet

castle gone
dreams of

childhood maple
mother's leaves

now gone
worms endeavor

in old nutrition
peace rose

once stood shaded
now gone

vines paint
walls stand

next to garden memories
and dreams

now gone

I Sit Listening

Listen
with quiet ears
so life
does not
unwillingly
pass you by.

A breath of story
blows over my past.

The indoor chimes
echo restless
in my windy mind.

Then, dawn comes;
I sit waiting
for the perfect image
to grow in my veins.

I see,
I am lighter today,
quieter today,
listening to the sounds of creation.

Perfect is not a song I know.
Still, I sit listening.

III

Behind Me—dips Eternity—
Before Me—Immortality—
Myself—the Term between—
Death but the Drift of Eastern Gray,
Dissolving into Dawn away,
Before the West begin—

EMILY DICKINSON

"I am Yours now, so please, take me
where you will, teach me about
eternity and other things of
consequence, carry me over the
remnants of a life I can barely
remember..."

JANAVI HELD

Original Body

They don't see
what lives underneath my eyes
or all the bodies I've inhabited
in this lifetime

My mother can see.
She remembers when my eyes were round,
so round and large taking in newness like water,
like nutrition.

But they, they don't see.
Do they imagine that I am elegant?
Neglecting to see that I was born
with a broken heart
whose broken bits keep falling
into other organs causing malfunction.
Today, those bits have reached my bones.

If they were blind,
would they see me more clearly?
Seeing with touch,
discovering lost bits of self leaping to the surface.

With their eyes and body language
they don't see all the past lives
that have shaped the karma
I drag reluctantly behind me today.
And they can't see the feeling I am afraid of
which tastes like insanity only on Sunday mornings.
They don't see my real shape and size,

they don't see what I really want to say,
they don't see the weeping in today's smile,
they don't see the way I touch the leaves and trees
when I walk in the arroyos.
They don't see the way that I giggle
when a flock of birds fly over head in perfect formation,
or my private altar,
and all the deities that live there,
or how I love the sky
because it is the color of God's skin.

They imagine
that this dress of bones, skin,
one heart, gray brain, some red liquid, etc.,
 is who I am.
They think my well-kept home
is an extension of my body;
they think comfort lives in my bank account
and in the talents that sustain my life,
but they don't know that these fallible soldiers scare me.

They could never guess
that I know the real names of the moon
and earth and sun, and how, sometimes at night,
I ask the silver globe of the moon
if it would cool my desires,
and if it would be at all possible
to go home now.
I even talk to the fabric maker of the atoms,
which compose this earth, asking him
to send a message through the chains of time and space,
so I may see, at least for a moment,
that which resides beyond this angry, gray cloud
where I stand today.

Whether they think
I am beautiful or ugly,
restless or committed,
talented or illegible,
kind or wicked—they are misinformed.
They can't remember, as I do,
that I have done all this before,
and because of this I am tired.
The kind of exhaustion
that is in danger of seeping into my timeless soul.
They don't understand
that I have had, already, too many
mothers and fathers, and sisters and brothers,
and husbands and wives, and friends and lovers,
and enemies and teachers, and masters and servants,
and every one of them has broken my heart
because they could not see my original body.

They do not understand
that I'm tired because
I've tried everything:
I was rich and powerful and cruel,
and I was poor and meek and kind,
and I have never found pleasure,
have never been able to sleep long enough to rest,
have never been well long enough to be sane,
have never been in love long enough to find You,
have never been able to talk loud enough to be heard,
have never been able to laugh loud enough to cry,
or cry hard enough to laugh.

So, in your eyes
I am in danger of staying encased
in that which is ever changing, yet stale.

Encased in perpetual death.
I am in danger of forgetting the cause of flocking birds,
and the color of God's skin,
and the feel of the leaves underneath my yearning fingers.

In your eyes
I am only liquid blood
and hard bone,
which when joined with the earth,
no one will remember.

What will become of me
if I imagine that blue is an illusion,
and the earth is my home?

What will become
of my ancestors
if I conclude
that I am made out of something
that resembles their bodies?

What will become of the souls
who have no memory,
or the innocence of children and flowers,
and sleeping things we never think to remember?

What will become of me
if these words dry up,
and my heart has no more tears for You?

If I am too long separated
from those who know my original name,
how will I get through the hours of my life without them?

What will become of me
if trees, so long spoken of,
have not the tolerance to recommend them?

What will become of me if
they never see the iron and steel I am made of,
which is melting gradually
into the shape of something divinely original.

And so, I tread silently
through the lies of these days.
Keeping You, my secret,
close at hand,
near my heart,
in the intelligent portions of my mind,
hoping that they will see me… someday.

And when we do touch,
as we feel those lost parts of self
leaping to the surface,
we will understand the original stuff
we are made of.

Prophecy

If you ask me for prophecy
That which cannot be seen
Between antiquity and time
I will become invisible
In the sad corners of my bedroom
Bewildered by a swarm of objects
With no mouths

They speak anyway
Of humiliated phantoms
And the smell
Of unanswered sacrifice
Like a thief
And with that same cold fever
They expand like drunken guests

At the foot of a mourner's bed.
The smell of rotten fruits
And the absence of light
Calls for the prophecy
To cease trembling
And singing to those
Indirect angels

As I drink the invisible water
As my bones settle
As the wind shutters
In my solitary mind
As something endless trembles
In the cavern of my chest
Speaking to the nascent ears

Of future blindness
I take those absent flowers
And press them to my eyes
Falling back into
The infinite substance of time
Burning my limbs
And prophesizing my drunken mind.

Forfeit

Her solitude wraps round her
like a lover, like God,

like an illness and its remedy,
like shattered stone,

like insatiable waves,
like the blunt flash of electricity

splintering the sky.
As her discarded heart fractures

wet hands of ruined fears
reach for the only One who will listen,

the One who hears
when all humans are dead,

when oxygen stops breathing,
and humiliated gravity has lost her power.

It is in this death of family
and all things impersonal

that she is seen at last
reaching for the invincible echo.

As she trembles with ending stories,
personalities, and discarded treasures,

she can no longer remember why
her eyes and hair are brown,

why she chose the burgundy curtains
that hang in her bedroom,

or why she prays for sleep on endless nights.
She can no longer see

her mother's face in her eyes
nor hear her father's deep voice in her mind;

she can't imagine who this is
as she stares at her reflection,

as she gazes through a pane of glass
at the blistering night sky

the history of the earth
shakes

in her solar plexus,
drops from her hands,

secretes from her skin:
splintering, dripping,

and mixing
with rock,

and thoughts,
and time—

and still she can't
remember a believable history,

can't imagine
why

she forfeited
the eternal sky.

Betrayal

What exterminators are these?
They devour clouds
Revealing more darkness
Cradling time
As if it were lightning
The servant of time
Whispers to frail flesh
As if she is a hero
She demands we arise
Once fallen
To fight for roots
In the plastic earth
Eternally collecting
Debits and credits.

Memory

I've walked so far
and gotten nowhere.
I contain endless memories
yet I own nothing.

My heart knows
the falling out
the falling down
the falling away

It remembers breaking
and dreams of ascending
and the endless labors
which daily life is famous for.

Titanic, lying memories
forfeiting time
lay in shards
at my feet.

My eyes clarify
without the nescience
of those terrestrial daydreams
and an ancient aria

I forgot to look for
shouts louder now
from the inside
of my temporary heart.

I Suffer from Not Knowing

Who are you
buried in the cyclone night,

destined to wake
with covered eyelids?

Are you shielded
by the terrified sky?

Or do you live transparent
in the invading moonlight?

Was it not for you
that the bell of spring rang,

and the circuits of summer heat
surrounded the memories of spring?

I suffer from not knowing truth,
cloistered in silence

away from the dampness of time,
from lips that would kiss you,

and the generous lies
that would reach you

with glacial arms,
white as oblivion.

I suffer from not hearing
the storm you wrote

when you lost the ancient loved one
and woke breathing blood, still dreaming.

But you remember the blue of the sky,
like monsoon clouds with reddish eyes

and lips like petals
of a moist lotus flower.

You've seen the pink palms
of those clouds,

the creased throat,
and the eternal feet dressed

in familiar symbols
of inevitable personality.

I suffer from not knowing
how the dream of separation

like an exiled widow,
shattered inside your heart,

fracturing eternal affection.

Here Today

Here today   and yet
I am so far behind my time.

Perhaps I will be caught   in a torrent of unyielding mercy
perhaps I will drown there.

And yet I wonder if I should believe
in this momentary renunciation

perhaps it's born of fever
some virus   quickening my blood

forcing my mind to submit
to the impending death of skin   and all things frail.

Perhaps I should not believe
that my hands have let go of romance   and money

although   all who have come thus far
are a pale comparison.

It's so simple now
and so obvious:

I don't want to circle round
in these shape-shifting bodies

I want to be   as I am   always
never losing collected treasures

never lying to breathe
never killing to eat.
It seems such a simple request
and yet   I still lie here

planning what color to paint
my prison walls.

Surgeon's Tools

I wish I had something to give You,
something that would surprise You
and make You smile, but today
You are my surgeon, for I am ill
sick with the disease of eons
transmigrated bacteria
tears at my bones, and You
are my only medicine.
Occasionally, I have the strength

to bring You dirt from my garden,
dead leaves, or discarded shells;
mostly I offer my titanic sorrow,
the address of orphaned tears,
or the publicist of my arrogance.
That arrogance, wrapped up
against my heart, shouts and swells
but cannot remember
the embarrassing lessons of yesterday.

I have been vigilant like a thief,
stealing away from You at night;
and in the dawn, I return
with shattered and burning fingers
from cavorting kindly with my enemies.
As I slip by You
into my silent bed,
I hear Your surgeon's tools
rattling in the dawn shadows.

Damage

I occupy my hours
as a surgeon,
a therapist,
a carpenter

remodeling a hurricane damaged home

nails stuck in wrong places,
shards of glass underfoot,
engorged and useless wood
laying sadly nearby

next to the ruination of everything;

and the foundation
has been uplifted,
flung to a distance

impossible to traverse from here.

How to begin,
when I am too poor
to purchase new materials?

Will I rebuild with twigs

from the forest floor
and build a roof
of grass and reeds?
Will there be

no furniture, no door, no privacy.

I can't remember
what that old house looked like
enough to judge
whether she was good or bad;

I only know that a strong wind came,

a wind laden with pride,
revealing the fragile nature of all things.
And yet I argue with that wind
that this one

built with the stones and stories of God

was supposed to last;
they told me it would last.

But the wind has her way.

And I am alone here
longing to be reassembled,

as the past walks the forest alone,

circles round the ruins,
and does not help
in the rebuilding,

does not lift even one brick or stone.

Soundtrack

The voice of friendship
speaks my soul
back to life
when I have spent
a night in lamentation.

And the sounds of the cresting sun
singing the moon and stars to rest
with her brilliant orange choirs.

And the river
restless, running,
shocking cold to tree roots
who rest and reach to her.

And those trees
velvet, golden, shape-shifting
aspens dancing
partnering with the wind,
their autumn song
prying my eyes and ears
away from sorrow.

They all chant and sing
to my broken open chest,
and in their music,
I neglect all the pain
which has chased me for years.

Pain's Purpose
In Three Parts

I

I've paid for healing
with bits of fragmented bone,
pools of depleted blood,

with the strands of flesh
kept closest to my heart,
with layers of seen inadequacy,

with the minutes of night,
and with the fatigue of daylight hours
fading like an irretrievable inheritance.

While purchasing healing
with the commodity of bad association
and labors unfit for a lady,

I've kept my night hours solemnly
bound to the visage of eternal time
silently remembered in my chest

those songs tell me
that only the contents of my heart
will last forever.

II

The scaffolding has fallen
from the surrogate building,
and form is a wraith

longing to be known
as temptation remembers
the false night into being

and tries to dress herself
in the glow of Venus,
yet she remains an apparition

whose short life flickers
in and out of being
at the whim of more

substantial architecture
hiding in the deep hours
of the transcendental night.

III

There is no pleasure
but the wind that spirit brings,
and the sun, like God's face,

warming my empty bones.
Despite my name
I am not a Hero,

do not have the strength
of wisdom, nor the rock
of humility to take another step.

I am a thief
stealing whatever nutrients I can
from the plants and milk of the earth,

as the hours pass
one into another,
and days with their fugitive minutes

lose their relevancy,
merging into the epoch of seasons,
and this shell cracks and seizes with age,

drying of old romantic notions,
and longing for the restless sweetness
at the end of time.

empty altars

i dream of empty altars
of eyes that won't touch me
of platters of sweets and savories

i have no stomach for

i clear piles of plates and trays
and when the exploitation
of the night is over

no eyes will touch me

in the light
i walk like a stranger
among old friends
and all the altars are empty

and no eyes will touch me

You are talked of
implied in whispered conversation
and all the altars are empty

and no eyes will touch me

The Lost Generation

I

There is a house
where the whole world
was meant to live.
I stand outside the gate,
looking for beloved relatives
and friends who have vanished
into a mess of civilization.
Here I remain exposed
to the violent elements of time
and fragmented desire,
with no structure
to house or perfect
my abilities
and disaffections.
Drifting,
I find you
in the swift river of need.

II

These burdens lay dark and heavy on my heart
as the rasping shrill of years
weaves them into a veil of mourning.
I see a trail of light
littering abandoned beings
who are drowning in a sea of perpetual death.
We cripple ourselves on these rocky shores of time,
as eternity travels, ceaseless, above.
I know a fresh tomb awaits me

among a host of tangled vegetation.
I know that my superstitious heart
lives among trees and fading flowers.
I know that without my friends
I am naked beneath
an avalanche
of mundanity.

III

I have no more bandages, no more needle and thread.
I only have this feeble canvas
I use to replace the past, and divine the future.
I have no present tense. It is taken in tears,
and replaced by a heartbeat,
which rolls slowly inside these mortal remains,
dressed in flesh, incarcerated in bone,
enduring the dead world,
searching for the minerals of life.
I speak of the humility of trees,
of the faithfulness of water, of patience,
of the nutrition of sacred sound,
of the sad attention of earthy days passing like smoke,
of constant angels, of sword-like knowledge.
I speak of the equality of spirit
and the disenfranchisement of matter,
the secondary nature of the mind
and the inconsistency and texture of emotion.
I speak, yet I am of a common color
living faithlessly like a coiled snake,
compact and suffocating in the oil of shadows.

IV

My disobedient soul sinks in the measureless night of smoke
and solitary walls. Yet, there is a transcendental sound,
which can dismiss this common darkness
penetrating this prepared universe
with a brusque cry of light.
It is a flare sent up from this shipwreck of being,
a banner of blue bringing wet to the dreary dryness of the desert
and the dehydrating salt of the ponderous sea.
Black as coal my heart has been put out to dry
in the arid winds. If observed closely,
the cruelty of a million years can be seen
dripping thick like tar from this essential muscle.
That black blood seeps into the earth,
begging for the sunrise to view this conquered twilight.

V

The thief of arrogance has stolen my essence
and I wander bloodless at dawn searching for You
in the corners of my mind
I examine the stagnating remains of remembered lives,
as so many names trade places in my nerves;
these fragments of forgotten lamentations doubling as truth
are drenched in the pallid weight of oblivion and memory.
I dig for You in these remains
as the very ether makes me weep
and the knife of separation is unforgiving.
Continuously, I am devoured by the sulfuric secrets I keep.
How is it possible to speak of Your beauty and lovely bright things
when the wretched stain of eons, like blades and exiled emptiness,
I have clutched within my greedy fingers?
Yet, by day the humbled remains of my heart
can be seen clearly

on the edge
of the weapon
of transcendental sound.

VI

As today's light pierces the horizon,
another year is dawning,
and I continue the search for my friends;
for us time does not pass in minutes
and so, we draw closer to home.

Saffron

I must take the back roads.
The well-trodden miles
do not suit
that which I was born to.

I have put aside
the monolithic crown of homogeny,
have a become a savage
for the sake of loving you.

I do not belong to man;
therefore, my beauty is ruthless
or how else will I come to know you
as the traditions collapse like dead trees

under a cold and infertile sky.
I will adopt any means
to reach across the barrier of birth
which separates our mortality

with the sword of knowledge
you've thrust into my hands;
I will pierce the blue of the sky
and take you home with me.

If I Were Dying

If I were dying, I would put away all distractions

Now, I watch the sun
from under my closed eyelids
as I rest in bed.
This is the luxury of today.

There have been so many minutes of living
that have felt like familiar death,
and just as time cries for me,
I know that luxuries do dry up,
and memory can be lost by new life.

Perhaps tomorrow
the whirlwind of weightless rain
will fall at my indifferent feet.
Perhaps, only hours—and the vacancy of minutes—
separate me
from that new, eternal sleep.

Today, pain is a subject which cannot be expanded.

If I falter,
if I keep stalling,
will you come back for me?

If I have loved beyond reason
and have lost the simple shape of things
will you still remember my name?

The face I wore when things were simple,
and progress was not this generational map,
and I couldn't help loving you?

If I were dying now, would you?

I didn't know that time could drag on like this,
through pain.
Still, I will not stop looking
at the sky outside my window…
this I can do.
Even, as I'm dying.

This Blue

Clarity

    like this blue

        above me,

and each strand of wind is seen perfectly,
each glimmering embellishment well met,

the center waits

           for exposure,
as breath becomes song,
              quietly.

A Little While Longer

Circling around
inside the privacy of time,
I seek a place to rest
with no payment due
and no walls,

a home where flowers grow
unattended,
and skin
does not become freckled
by the sun.

I am burned here,
without a promise that
I may lay my head
on the grass
where Eternity has walked,

so that I will sleep at last
without the nightmare of time
tricking my personality
into gaining possessions,
into carrying the burdens of the phoenix,

into owing so much to so many.
To survive in time
I must earn
and fight
against the creeping pain

whose tentacles
have grown so long now

that there is not blood or breath.
Sometimes, I imagine it is black,
a bluish black like clouds in June,

and at these times,
I am not afraid of being smothered by it.
Let it come! Even in my dreams!
For if I could think of anything,
have anything,

that would remind me of You,
I could bear all this walking,
and thinking, and earning,
for just a little while longer.
Just a little while longer.

Out of Time

Today I remember
ether, falling through space
with no destiny.

Today I feel
that breath is an illusion
whose time will run out.

Today I see that I am running
out of breath
and time
and space.

In time,
all will be betrayed:
skin and bones—
so well kept
for all these years—
will give in
to the perishable
elements.

Out of time.
There is no
betrayal.

I Don't

I don't want to know the whereabouts of God, or the science of the cosmos
or the philosophy spoken by those who are paid to speak.
I don't want to know cause and effect, or become well-studied in
the endless punishments of this ephemeral prison.

I must disregard the linear flow of this temporal place,
because it forces unnatural philosophy on me,
makes me think that death is real and God is not mine,
not even a distant relative.

I see I have trespassed here long enough,
played with the toys, and carried the burden of endlessness.
By the ravages of time I have been stripped down to nothing,
stood before Eternity at noon and begged to be conquered.

Yet, the mortal river does not wake me in this well-guarded night,
only the loud clashing of my wasted efforts rouses my ire
as I drink the poison I have brewed for generations together.

I am not interested in discovering the whereabouts of God,
unraveling the mysteries of time and space,
or the words of those who juggle the names of eternity
with mercenary intentions.

As the sun sinks on another body and bardo awaits,
what will I speak there to the nascent ears of darkness,
to that momentary forest night?
Will I regret the generations spent without

 the sanctity of prayer on my lips,
worshipping that transitory master
who seems to speak with the tongues of the paragon?
I am not interested in discovering the whereabouts of God,
nor will I attempt to unravel the mysteries of time and space,

nor the words of those who juggle the names of eternity
with mercenary intentions.

I hold onto the toys of this place
as if I am a robot controlled from without,
but I am an adult now;
I wish to graduate to permanent toys,

no longer wasting time with finite games,
no more sand castles,
no more flowers that grow for a season
only to fertilize more temporary roses.

Can I be an eternal rose in a perennial garden,
or a blade of grass, or reeds winding through
the loving branches of desire-trees?
Can I watch the eternal dance from a distance,

discovering the immortality of a constant heart?
May I come home after gentle labors
to find the tiny footsteps of Eternity
waiting for me where I sleep?

Or am I the unlucky one
who is destined to sleep for all time?
Will I ravage love until nothing is left to offer?

And today I don't want to know philosophy,
or God, or the science of the cosmos,
or what happens after this unnatural death.

If I must stay in the green branches of temporary trees,
may I be allowed the dignity of a deep sleep,
where I may dream of the dark limbs of ageless time
and the words of the saints I can no longer hear.

When I wake, just momentarily, for the nutrition of my body,
let me find the remnants of my sister's feasts

to fill me with affection during my vision quest,
during the remaining dregs of this infernal disaffection.

I am not interested in discovering the whereabouts of God,
unraveling the mysteries of time and space,
nor what happens after this unnatural death.

Everything

Its left ugly behind
the emergence,
butterfly, phoenix.
Its face is gold
delighted.
Its hair a rainbow,
sudden after
the soul-drenching storm.
A child barely speaking,
saying everything.

Wake Now!

Wake now!
Dawn is rising from her ancient sleep,
never seen before.

Can't close eyes to it,
staring unbound at eastern chivalries.

Cool, cool sun only now, be present.
And suddenly its pinnacle crests the blue atmosphere,
and arid heat, and light, tucks me inside her earth.

Break

There will be   A better version   When the cocoon breaks

And the shell falls   And the glass slips   Shattering to the floor.

When the old bottle is empty   When time no longer drags

When lightning stops dancing

                        And desire is heard in the rain.

I Desire

I desire
to stand where time
can no longer see me
and write for You forever
about the things I can't understand now
and the love that is invisible to me
about Your beauty
which I cannot see.

Rules

There is
a restless beauty
in the winds
of simple despair

sands of time
shatter
no matter what
age or time
grabs what wills you

stamp out
the cold fire
of rules:
those foolish things
blocking creative forces
always
to be reckoned with.

Safety
never makes
true things.
Even in minds
saturated with brilliance.

Step differently—
finding your gait,
opening new worlds
where you stand
with love,
out of reach
of old monsters.

Not fighting
just stepping
to the side
where people live,
knowing the difference
in bones
of fearless
self-made lives.

Dress

I dressed like those who worshipped You
Put all the proper markings on my body

I walked and moved and talked like them
But I always knew I was lying

Eventually, I was swept away
On one long night that became many days

But something strange occurred
As those unkept years languished by

Something new came in my mind
I found my own dress, and markings, and speech

That resemble, just a little, of what they meant to teach
It sprang from somewhere that feels like You

And feels like me
And today, I have no care

For what I wear
When I think of You.

Freedom

Every day, my day
a monument to the Divine
and I am speaking freedom
I am inside freedom
my life sits
inside the palm of the universe
peeling back those fingers
which are the organs
of trees and leaves
my life escapes limits
as old roads self-demolish
as I seep into everything
that owns the name freedom.

There Is a Shore

Portals rest
on far away shores.
With brown eyes watching
mermaids appear
from plankton
and weeds from graves of minerals,
and seal songs
come
trapping a longing
that once sat on your chest.
In your open hand,
it spoke to you
and flooded
your cells with a stampede
of turning memories
and stories,
which could not be contained
in your small palm.

Vast is my eyes' reach,
now that experience
has learned all about me.
It has learned
how to lick my life clean
of all symbols
and vows made
by another body
in another life.

There is a shore:
its memory is of golden tides
and silver waters.

Touching that ocean
with mortal hands,
it turns to milk
and drinks
your memories,
as it washes over
your infant-ways—
what you used to be
before you forgot
your heart
in this slow river
of living.

Sacred River

My namesake
flows through a land
I have never seen,
but which feels like home.

She is a river
full of mercy
and feminine waves,
in control of the destinies
on her banks,
of her people's future.

She cannot be contained
by dams.

In her,
sacred dancing myth
and true stories collide.

Bravery lives in her waters,
and kindness
washes up
on her pale shores.

My namesake
flows through a land
I have never seen,
but which feels like home.

I Wish I Had Wings

I wish I had wings!
I'd leave this prison
of gravity behind
and go up and up,
grazing the tops of
dazzling green trees,
swaying in the wind.

I'd soar through
the mists of bright clouds
breathing in freedom,
and moist particles
of fog and rain.

I'd turn my face
to the sun:
warm…
warming
my insides,
breaking the prison
of flesh and bone
wide open

I'd bathe in sweet
moon rays
and drink
the dust of stars
filling my heart
with ancient light.

I'd look down
at the swarming
Earth, but I'd never
look back.

After

After faint hopes
And long vigils.
After eternal loss
And protected ashes.
After wood
And dead ships
In the night.
After testimony
To affirm worship.
After oblivion
And quantity.
After enduring days
And impossible nights.
After time's funeral
And fugitive shadows,
Science, and weapons,
And weeping.
After glorious twilights
And perfume.
After wavering children.
After the edge of resistance.
After loud destruction.
After the silver of ceremony.
After bedrooms
And the uniforms of trees,
Tranquility, and thirsty lips,
And complicated substance,
And human beings
And nowadays
And clothes
And arms and legs.
After smoke and sand.

After lamentations
And degraded doubts.
After death
What?
After constant victory
And perpetual failure.
After the increase and decrease
Of populations,
And the circulation of darkness.
After propaganda
And human armies.
After accumulating,
And rotating, and solitude.
After witness, and execution,
And night returning.
After fusion,
A portrait,
A sunken face,
A cold wind.
After expansions
And extensions.
After the depths
Of desertion.
After faithful widows,
And mud,
And overturned intentions.
After death,
What?
After the rotation of the multitudes
And bodies of chaos.
After cruelty and punishment.
After pomegranate mornings,
And harvest nights,
And the buildings like mountains.
After today,
What?

After residence,
And passage,
And deciphered nothings.
After geography and empty isolation.
After ancestors and religions.
After violent mourning.
After the dust.
After the unspoken sings.
After the fire.
After awakening love,
What?
After the drunken bones of intoxication.
After repetition, repetition, after repetition
What?
After desecrating the dead,
And celebrations,
And enlightenment,
 and clear water,
And the slaves of time.
After farewells,
And tears,
And engraved guns,
And the bloody altars of eons.
After invasions
And humbled nations.
After slaves and murders,
And the eyelids of blindness.
After mirrors
And mortality.
After pity.
After martyrdom,
And serpents,
And the demolished ashes of the rose.
After the immortality of stars
And the fire of avarice, the corpse,
The spared day, the sterile seconds,

Dampness and tools.
After the city,
And the fearful weight of naked time.
After vanity and wine.
After laughter
And after dying,
What?
After the immunity of innocence.
After the determination of greed.
After lust.
After the dance is done.
After healing.
After shaking loose.
After karma.
After eternity.
After
Life,
After
Death,
After
Life,
After
Death,
What?

"Death must be so beautiful. To lie in the soft brown earth, with the grasses waving above one's head, and listen to silence. To have no yesterday, and no tomorrow. To forget time, to forgive life, to be at peace."

OSCAR WILDE

Afterword

Wind (a short fairy tale)

In a fit of wisdom, I plunged out of the bed of idleness into the frost snow biting my bare feet with memory. My breath, hot on the cold air, begged for iron hands to rip open the steel cage containing a treasure I have never seen. I wanted to be free. I was like a child, like a child, I thought: wild and curious and longing for inspiration and strong feet, that I may follow the wind in her relentless path over the endless surfaces and features of the earth. I found the wind when I was too young to speak. It told me stories of everything that it had encountered, and I became lost in those tales. That may have only been the fiction of a local wind, longing for freedom, as I did too. There was also a wind from India, carrying the smell of exotic spices and perfumed smoke; a wind that smelled of coal and English roses and…

I wonder where I've been born.

Janavi Held

"And if death is death,
what will become of poets?
and things in a cocoon
which no one remembers?"

FEDERICO GARCÍA LORCA
(1898 –1936)

(Excerpt from Janavi's favorite poem)

About the Author

JANAVI HELD (1965–2018)—originally born Judith Claudine Held, was an artist, dancer, photographer, yogini and poet originally from Brooklyn. A very sensitive, imaginative and receptive child, Janavi was captivated by nature, and alternative learning styles. The daughter of publishers and the niece of Joseph Heller—author of the bestselling classic, *Catch-22*—Janavi was raised to love books, despite having struggled with dyslexia.

Janavi started writing her own poetry and wandering around with her father's camera as a child. She was a very gentle, yet adventurous spirit. In 1984, at the age of nineteen—while a student at Naropa University—Janavi began practicing Bhakti Yoga. She eventually graduated with honors from Goddard College (2005-2009) where she studied poetry, photography, and media studies. Just as her bourgeoning career as a writer and professional photographer was peaking, Janavi fell gravely ill.

Bedridden in the last years of her life, Janavi processed the intense physical pain that characterized her illness through spontaneously immersing herself in artistic and spiritual growth. During this "renaissance of her soul" she authored *Letters to My Oldest Friend: A Book of Poetry and Photography* (Krishna West Inc., 2017) and contributed poems to two poetry anthologies, *Bhakti Blossoms: A Collection of Contemporary Vaishnavi Poetry* (Golden Dragonfly Press, 2017), and *Goddess: When She Rules—Expressions by Contemporary Women* (Golden Dragonfly Press, 2018). Two of Janavi's poems were also shortlisted for the prestigious Hamilton House International Poetry Prize awarded by the University Centre Grimsby, and published in their anthology *Eternal* (Hammond House, 2017).

After several years of searching for, and exploring healing solutions and treatments, while primarily cared for by her sister Sue, Janavi passed away at the age of 53, on December 8, 2018. She left behind an eclectic collection of work spanning across various mediums of expression, including artistic photography, cinematography, essays, short stories, digital art, and especially, poetry. Janavi's voluminous literary oeuvre consists of over four thousand poems, some which appear in this collection of poetry: *Whispers from Her Deathbed*. You may read more of Janavi's poems and view her artwork, including her digital collages, on www.janaviheld.com

Editor

CATHERINE L. SCHWEIG founded Journey of the Heart: Women's Spiritual Poetry in 2012, an online project from which five anthologies emerged, the latest titled *Goddess: When She Rules* (Golden Dragonfly Press, 2018). Catherine was a very dear friend of Janavi's, who communicated very closely with her in the years leading up to her demise. Catherine serves on the board of the Janavi Held Endowed Poetry and Art Grant. She and her husband live near the Powhatan River, and together mentor students in ahimsa living via ancient yoga psychology and philosophy.

Cover Artist

LANDIS BLAIR is the author and illustrator of *The Envious Siblings: and Other Morbid Nursery Rhymes*, as well as the illustrator of the *New York Times* bestseller *From Here to Eternity* and the graphic novel *The Hunting Accident*, which won the 2021 Fauve d'Or and the 2020 Quai des Bulles prize. He has published illustrations in numerous print and online periodicals including *The New Yorker*, the *New York Times*, *Chicago* magazine, *VQR*, and *Medium*. He lives in Chicago.

Acknowledgements

I wish to extend my heartfelt gratitude to all those who contributed to the production of this book: Firstly, to my dearly departed friend Janavi, for having entrusted me with the beautiful bounty of poetry she produced throughout her life. I am deeply honored. To Janavi's godmother, Marcia Newfield, who gave Janavi her first book of poems, ever encouraging her to write. To Janavi's spiritual teacher, H.D. Goswami, who resuscitated Janavi's creative voice, even as her body withered, and published her first poetry collection: *Letters to My Oldest Friend* (Krishna West, Inc. 2017.) To Janavi's sister, Sue Held, for having been Janavi's primary caretaker in her last years, facilitating Janavi's creative expressions—the flow of her art and poetry. To Nidra Patterson—through whom I first met Janavi—who acted as Janavi's loving spiritual mother and death doula, until her last breath. To Brian Bloch, who assisted us in securing Janavi's digital poetry files which were on the verge of being lost to cyberspace. To published poet and author, my dear friend, Carolyn Casas, who brought her sensitive assistance, competence and editorial suggestions to the manuscript. To talented author and illustrator Landis Blair, a pleasure to collaborate with, who brilliantly and carefully manifested my vision of the book's cover into a reality, exceeding my expectations. To my dear friend Alice—the magic behind Golden Dragonfly Press—for her ever-diligent, all-around skillful work and guidance, and for coordinating the release of this book with Janavi's birthday. And, to my beloved life-companion and husband, Graham, who offered me his warm and loving, essential support throughout the process of painstakingly piecing this book together, while grieving its author. Lastly, I deeply thank each of you—friends, mentors, relatives, students and teachers of Janavi—who inspired her unique creative process throughout her life, contributing to this nourishing flow of poetry that now outlives her.

Made in the USA
Middletown, DE
08 June 2022

66629839R10085